Closing C

MW00942059

How to ~~Be a Bold Leader~~ and Develop a Kick-Ass, High-Functioning, Happy AF Team

Lynne Maureen Hurdle
The Conflict Closer

Dedication

This book is dedicated to:

God for every single step I have taken to make this book a reality.

My mom Eleanor Blassingame Hurdle whose remedy for when my sister and I were bored was "get a book and read." Thank you mom.

My dad David Leroy Hurdle who told me "anything boys can do you can do too."

My sister Leslie Gayle Hurdle my first and forever best friend.

My sons Jabari and Justin Nai'im who are genuinely proud of me and make me genuinely proud every day.

To my niece Sekai who is always interested in knowing what new thing I am up to lately.

To my husband Warren Price and my mother-in-law Marie Price who never stopped believing in me.

To my cousin Monet who knows the good, the bad and the ugly.

To all of my clients who put their trust in me and my work and encouraged and pushed me to "write a book already."

To my family and friends who have always encouraged me to live my dreams.

Foreword

I'm a little biased, I confess.

Lynne Maureen Hurdle was my boss in the early 90's. My instant thought is dang, that was a really, really long time ago. It was. We were in the resolving conflict business. Lynne headed a Training Division for the Victim Services Agency in Manhattan. We trained young people in the New York City Public School System and some of their teachers to become mediators. We helped them set up mediation centers. I was one of Lynne's trainers and received my Mediation Training from attorneys at the Brooklyn Courts. The sort of cases that Judge Judy peddles on television, they used to be handled by mediators like me at the court, back in the days.

So we knew a thing or two about resolving conflict. It WAS a long time ago. But what I remember most vividly from that period are our staff meetings. Yes, really. The staff meetings. Because we spent our weekdays in the trenches, training students in far-flung schools throughout New York City, we held our staff meetings every other Friday afternoon, from 3 to 5 pm, at our main office in Manhattan, catty-cornered from City Hall. 3 pm on a Friday, at the end of a bruising work week. That's crazy. Like really crazy, right?

We had energized meetings. And Lynne Maureen Hurdle is the best boss I have ever had, hands down.

Here's why. And here's what I learned about leadership in those meetings. It all connects to conflict.

- **Find time to have real conversations**. That means time for conversations that are not rushed and allowed to breathe a little. Conversations where we can settle into our topics. Conversations that are more than let's-get-through-the-agenda marathons. Conversations that create space for a bit of conflict to bubble up.

- **Invite conflict.** Make it explicit that conflict is welcome. Consider it one of your meeting norms. Actively invite it. If necessary, play devil's advocate to court it. Demand multiple perspectives. Champion disagreement. Yes, celebrate the heck out of it.

- **Dive in**. That means when conflict rises to the surface, resist the urge to squelch or contain it. Trust that your group is strong enough to disagree. Have faith that the heated emotions which may arise will subside, and that unlocking disagreement is a potent way of getting out of stasis and moving forward.

The single most important success factor in our meetings? Tired as we were on a Friday afternoon, we began each meeting with a 15-minute playful icebreaker. An experiential game, often physical. High-spirited, fun. The icebreaker switched us from our brains back into our bodies. It put us into a good mood. It propelled us into whatever conversation we needed to have with a playful spirit. It enabled us to "do conflict" in a more lighthearted manner.

This is a norm in all I do, to this day. So simple. Yet here is something I experience all too often in my role as a C-Suite coach. A client will invite me to observe an executive meeting so I may get a first-hand sense of group dynamics. Especially if the meeting gets a little messy, my client is wont to apologize afterwards. I am so sorry you had to see that.

That piece of the meeting was, of course, invariably the very best part. Things got real. Conflict happened. Yes, it got a little messy. Hallelujah.

I like the term "Conflict Closer." Back in the days we called it conflict resolution, but I prefer the allusions of the word "Closer." It doesn't suggest that we always resolve everything. It may mean that two sides get closer to each other. I prefer closeness to distance. It may mean that, like a sales person, we close a deal. Close it without figuring it all out, perhaps. Close it and agree to accept our differences when it comes to some things.

That's the grown-up conflict stuff. "Revel in this little book. Inhale its wisdom. Lynne Maureen Hurdle is a pioneer who has been working in the conflict closing vanguard for over three decades. She knows. And after reading this book, so will you. And that's a beautiful thing."

– Achim Nowak, Business Thinker/TEDx Speaker/ Mastermind Convener and International Authority on Embodied Leadership

Table of Contents

Introduction

I grew up watching Emma Peel on the TV show, The Avengers. Everything she did, from walking into a room to handling a difficult conversation and delivering a fierce side-kick, she did with extreme confidence. The impact she had on me was here was a woman who knew that she was highly skilled in talking to people in any conflict situation and thus chose to take it to the extreme (in her case using martial arts) only when her life was in danger.

With all the conflict that is happening and with every major business magazine and journal reporting about the importance of leaders building healthy relationships and diverse, high functioning teams, social skills are fast becoming the primary tools for success. Those who will be most successful in making major and impactful changes are those leaders willing to be **Bold** when it comes to dealing with conflict.

Bold Leaders know that they must skilfully and willingly engage in conflict, because it is both inevitable and necessary. Conflict can bring new ideas, opinions and perspectives to the workplace, leading to healthy conversation, invested team members, increased productivity and profits. However, this only happens if we as leaders are confident in our ability to face conflict, engage in it and manage it.

Bold Leaders anticipate and set the table for conflict, with the mind-set that discussing the root causes of a conflict before it blows up only makes everyone's job much easier. That means that we run into the fire of conflict while others are busy filming it or running the other way.

A crucial and yet often missed point is that **Bold Leaders** continuously go within themselves to search for and own up to what they do to escalate conflict. We all have the potential to escalate conflict because we all have triggers. Triggers are fueled by emotions which set off reactions rather than responses. **Bold Leaders** know that in order to take triggers off of their plate, they must examine their own feelings towards conflict and discover the root causes.

One of my favorite leadership stories is told by Dan Gilbert, owner of the Cleveland Cavaliers. In an interview with Forbes Magazine, he discussed his conflict with LeBron James, which arose when LeBron announced in a not-so-nice way that he was leaving the Cavaliers and going to the Miami Heat. Gilbert admits that he "went off" in a very public manner. "I can have a short fuse at times …

I can't believe I actually went off like that… I might be right about what I felt, but I should have taken half an hour to think about it first." He thoughtfully recalls that receiving praise and accolades for his bad behavior kept him from really evaluating it for quite some time. However, once he took the time to examine the scenario, he was forced to go within himself and discover a part of him that needed some work. He learned some hard but good lessons about his emotional reaction. Doing the work prepared him to get past that embarrassing moment and allowed him to reach out to LeBron to work things out. At that in-person meeting, the first words he said were, "we had five good years and one bad night."

LeBron's response? "Apology accepted."

That is **Bold Leadership.** I'm guessing that you want to be that kind of leader and that's why you are taking your valuable time to read this book.

Who Am I?

I am Lynne Maureen Hurdle, known as The Conflict Closer, a conflict resolution and communication coach who works with high achieving leaders.

These **Bold Leaders** know that they want to be on top of their competition when it comes to high performing, productive teams and excellent customer service. And the way there is through tight conflict resolution—actively communicating, engaging in, and resolving conflict."

I fell into this conflict resolution gig so unexpectedly and yet it was also divinely purposed. In 1975, I was 17 years old and living with my parents and my older sister in the Bronx. I rode the city bus to and from school and one day, when I was about a mile away from home, I noticed that the city bus driver did not open the doors when we pulled up to a bus stop. I looked through the front window and saw a mob of young white males wearing red bandannas on their heads charging towards us. They looked to be around 50 in number. They surrounded the bus and started screaming that they were going to get the Ni***rs. It was right at this moment that I noticed two things that terrified me.

First was that, the bus driver, a teenage male and myself were the only black people on the bus.

The second thing was their baseball bats, which they were using to hit the sides of the bus while demanding that we come out.

When the bus driver held his ground and refused to open the door, the mob began to try and tip the bus over. The only thing that saved us was the arrival of another bus across the street filled with African-American teenagers. The mob ran across the street and I jumped off the bus with the other teenager. He was terrified, not only because of this horrifying incident but also because this was his first week living in this area.

Welcome to the neighbourhood kid.

I took him to his place and then walked home from there (we still stay in touch to this day. Let's face it, we had quite an introduction!). I remember thinking of only one thing as I walked home, "I don't know how, but I have to do something with my life that brings people together around these situations."

From the time I was five years old, I knew that I wanted to be an entertainer. I danced, sang and acted from childhood. I even started writing plays, songs, poems and fictional stories when I was 8 years old. Therefore, at 17, my goal was to go to an excellent university that had a prestigious theater program. I had no idea where this 'save the world and help people deal with conflicts' idea came from. I was going to be a star! I did get accepted to Syracuse University as a theater major. However, in my junior year, I abruptly switched to their new Non-Violent Conflict and Change major.

I wasn't even close to God back then, but I believed that somebody knew something about my future regardless of whether or not that something was part of my plans.

Since then, I've invested over 35 years into conflict resolution where I have helped people work through unresolved conflict soulfully and effectively. I've worked with clients from the South Bronx to South Africa and from Harlem to Hong Kong. My secret sauce is the fact that I have been using everything I teach my clients in my own life. I'm a wife, a mother, a CEO, a friend, and so much more. In every one of these roles, I encounter conflict, choose to engage and resolve it.

Well, not every time, but that's the secret ingredient to the secret sauce, it's not always about whether it was resolved every time, but rather how you engage every time.

As for that Kick-Ass, High-Functioning, Happy AF Team? I hired, supported, motivated and boldly led one for several years using much of what I am going to tell you about in this book. Lucky for you, I have learned a lot since then and I'm going to include some of that too.

Now, let's talk about you for a minute. I may not know YOU, but here are some things that I know for sure:

Leaders want to have a positive influence over their teams, clients, followers and even their haters.

Businesses that have influence, impact and longevity all start and end with leaders who have the skills to respond precisely, powerfully and professionally in conflict situations.

Developing that influence starts with becoming a **Bold Leader** and creating a Kick-Ass, High-Functioning, Happy AF Team.

And that starts with YOU getting comfortable with conflict.

Why You Should Listen to Me

I have already told you that during the course of these thirty plus years, I have travelled the world helping leaders in many different arenas. One thing I learned from the multitude of diversity out there is that, when it comes to really leading people, most leaders are faking it, including the many financially successful leaders. While they are faking it or failing at it, many teams are suffering, which is bad for business.

Too many leaders are firing people unnecessarily, getting into endless arguments with their team, and showing up for meetings where no one can admit their mistakes for fear of being humiliated. And leaders are leaving those meetings frustrated, confused and venting to the few leaders they can trust, who are having the same difficulties with their teams.

Yet, the face these leaders show to the public is one of "I have it all together" because they have no choice. They throw money at business coaches, brand strategists, copy writers and financial wealth building courses. These are all good investments, but none of them can address what every leader needs to get masterful at: Conflict, especially closing conflict.

I didn't always deal with conflict the way I do now. I started out by learning about mediation, negotiation and conflict resolution techniques and then presenting workshops, keynotes and seminars with leaders in the worlds of education and business. I also tried very hard to 'walk the talk' in my personal life.

There was always something missing though. People would learn a lot; they would even start using some of the skills they learned in the role-plays that I would have them do. Nonetheless, when it came to implementing the skills in their work to deal with conflict, they resorted to their old ways of avoidance, yelling or threats. Many would come back for repeat workshops or advanced seminars. In the end, they were still not using the skills they had learned or becoming as proficient as they needed or wanted to be.

It wasn't until I became a mother that I began to unravel the mystery behind this. By far too many of us in the business world believe that business and personal are separate entities and that you can leave your personal self at the door when you enter the business world. I am here to tell you that there is absolutely a connection between what you do in your personal life and what you do in business when it comes to conflict and communication.

Believe me, you do not leave your triggers, emotions and conflict history at the door when you step into work. You may be able to hide it or repress it for a while, but it is still there, unleashing thoughts, filtering what you hear, changing what you believe about others and generally affecting the way you interact with others in the world of work. Therefore, when I tell you that my work started to transform because of what was happening in my personal life, I need you to understand that the connection was strong.

I spent the early part of 1994 watching my mom waste away and suffer from what was later discovered as the return of breast cancer. By July, she was unexpectedly and unbearably gone. BAM! And I was hit from behind.

The chance to experience what so many parents experience, or what ecstatic grandparents experience when they wait to lovingly "spoil" a child, was a dream I'd held for so many years. I'd admired watching my mom fuss over everyone else's grandchildren as she longingly and desperately waited to hold her own.

A year later our son came bursting into our lives and the joy kept me from drowning in the depression I had sunk into after the loss of my mother. My mom was gone and she could no longer answer all the parenting questions I had planned to ask her. I was lost. Even though there were so many things she did as a mother that I disliked, I still ached for her to fill that role.

When I finally stopped crying, I had a terrifying and liberating thought: As a new mother, who was parenting without her mother, I could harness the power of that freedom and make new rules.

With that freedom, I began to look into conflict in a deeper manner. I started with discipline and what I had been taught about it and then extended it to examining the relationship I had with conflict. It was a good thing too because six years later, when my next son was born, my life really changed, and conflict became a regular occurrence. It's not that my oldest son did not provide plenty of opportunities to confront conflict, it's just that he was less in love with it and we saw more things eye to eye. My second son came into the scene questioning and pushing back on just about everything and everyone while having the nerve to be incredibly likeable and enjoyable. On top of all of this, my husband either avoided or exploded during conflict. I had a real team to learn from.

Here's the deal though… my biggest lessons about conflict came from what I was learning about myself. When I began applying those lessons to my work, my clients started having extreme transformations. I began by inviting them to learn more about conflict. I call it "Getting Intimate with Conflict." I helped them explore "The Soul of Conflict"—the place where old conflict wounds reside. I taught them to identify and acknowledge the effect it had within them. I then assisted them to work through their feelings, release them and make the necessary changes to end its effects.

The results were amazing!

Now I always use this as the starting point, and when I combine it with techniques, strategies and my own experiences, leadership transformation happens. My clients like *Sandy, *Thomas and *Tamara can tell you. They have each given me permission to share some of their transformation stories because they want you to know how this work can benefit you.

If you want to know how to be a **Bold Leader** with influence, with a Kick-Ass, High-Functioning, Happy AF Team, and how to engage in conflict skillfully, confidently and powerfully, then you need to keep reading.

How to Use This Book

You will start to notice as you read this book that I have packed a lot in to it. Although it is all practical and useful it can be a lot to digest at one time. I encourage you to put the book down after each chapter and take some time to think how you can apply what you've just read to yourself and your team. It's ok if you feel like you not only want help applying this on a consistent basis, but that you also want more. That's why my clients come to me for coaching. This book is a real starting place for change whether conflict resolution is new to you or been something you've incorporated in to your leadership style already. Take your time, BREATHE. Breathing properly and regularly is such an important part of the work. Taking care of yourself and being kind but relentlessly curious when you make mistakes is crucial. Then keep going back to read and practice and keep this book handy because it will be useful to you in your next conflict.

Chapter 1

What Do I Mean by Closing Conflict?

The truth about conflict is, most of us don't like it or want anything to do with it and some of us even run from it. Conflict is really about communication and as a leader, you do that every day. You just need your words and actions to have their intended impact on others. This will in turn help them hear you, understand your vision, get inspired by you and be moved to action in even the most difficult situations. That's the kind of action that creates happiness, longevity and profits.

Difficult situations and conflict in general however bring up a lot of negative feelings for leaders because, as the one in charge, you know that ultimately, conflict is going to reach your door and you are going to be expected to do something about it. Most leaders try to put off that day of reckoning for as long as possible, which only fosters resentment, frustration and escalation of the conflict.

If we are to effectively engage in and close conflict, we need to tackle it on two levels. The first is within ourselves and the second is with those who are either in conflict with us or with others on our team.

Let's start with the first level of closing conflict. We don't come out of a conflict clean. Instead, we carry our conflict stories—the stories about how we were first introduced to conflict and all of the unresolved conflicts that we still harbor feelings for. Of course, if we've had successes with solving conflict, we carry those successes with us as well, but science has proven that our brains are wired to alert us to and protect us from danger and therefore hold on to negative experiences longer.

In one of the numerous studies done on this topic, John Cacioppo, Ph.D., demonstrated that, "the brain, reacts more strongly to stimuli it deems negative. There is a greater surge in electrical activity. Thus, our attitudes are more heavily influenced by downbeat news than good news." (https://www.ncbi.nlm.nih.gov/pubmed/9825526) We then hold on to those experiences and they create the stories we both unconsciously and consciously tell ourselves about our lives, and in particular, about conflict.

So many of us have had negative experiences with conflict. If we are to close conflict, we've got to discover those stories, something I call 'the roots of conflict in our lives.' We have to work harder in order to bring them to the surface. We then have to examine them and develop an awareness of how they affect us during conflict situations. I know that sounds like a lot. I'm not going to lie, this work never ends, but I can show you how surfacing and developing an awareness of just one unresolved conflict can set you up to discover others easily. This leads to greater and quicker awareness and transformation.

The Conflict Closer Weighs In: Meet *Sandy

*Sandy decided to work with me in my Leadership C.O.R.E. Program. She signed on because she realized that, like many entrepreneurs, she jumped into building her business and started becoming successful and building a team, but when conflicts increased within her business, she didn't have the leadership tools to handle them the way she wanted to. She wanted to unapologetically lead with confidence, skill and compassion, but had no real training in this before she bravely started her business.

Our work began with her telling me about her Conflict Story. Through that sharing, I helped her *become aware of her major and unresolved childhood conflict of abandonment. In uncovering this, we were able to unpack a recent reaction she had to some statements made by one of her team members during a conflict. She was able to connect her inner reaction of thoughts of "she's not loyal and may leave" to her unresolved conflict story of abandonment. I helped her recognize that her abandonment story created triggers for her, which led to her categorizing these statements as not being loyal when in reality, it might not have anything to do with that. We were able to prepare for further communication with the team member where she in fact learned that loyalty was not the issue. Here's the kicker... As a result of bringing that unresolved conflict to the surface, she was able to catch herself whenever she tried to relate an issue of loyalty to any conflict scenarios with others and make the shift to listening more rather than reacting. She found herself much more trusting of her team because she was less triggered by thinking that they were going to leave her whenever conflict arose.*

The bonus was that she found herself becoming aware of other parts of her conflict story that triggered her during different conflict situations and put the strategies that I had taught her to work to begin to investigate and remove those triggers.

The more aware we are, the more strategies and tools we implore, and the less impact these unresolved conflicts have on us. That's the work of bringing conflict close and closing conflict.

To start your own work on your conflict story ask yourself these three questions.

How did the people who raised you handle conflict?

What did that teach you about conflict?

How does that show up when conflicts arise?

Building A Strong Leadership C.O.R.E. In my business, I have learned that your business is only as healthy as your relationship and communication with your team. The key to Closing Conflict and Developing A Kick Ass, High-Functioning, and Happy AF teams is learning to lead from a strong **C.O.R.E.:**

Communication

Objectivity

Resolving Conflicts

Executing Excellence

Most of us know that when it comes to our body, our core is our strength. It supports every other part of our physical make-up. It is the same in leadership. We need our core strength to help us create strong teams that support every aspect of our business.

Most leaders forget that your team is not just resources; they are people with skills, talents and yes, feelings. They need a leader who knows how to capitalize on these features in ways that motivate, nurture and move them to happily execute the vision for the company and the team. Many businesses have "people working for them," while others have "teams in name only" but what I am talking about is different. A Kick-Ass, High-Functioning, Happy AF team understands how the mission, reputation and relationships contribute to the success of a business. Each member of the team knows their importance to the business and feels like they are part of a family that knows who they are, cares about them as individuals inside and outside of their work and is committed to their success alongside the success of the business.

I started out in the theater world where I participated both on-stage and backstage. The best experiences I had were the ones where I knew that the sound effects I was responsible for were as important to the show as the lead actress's monologue. Every role worked together to make a successful production.

This is the kind of team that I am talking about. In this team, every person knows that they have a skillful, confident, and powerful leader and that they have a hand in making the business run well, no matter what their role is. And guess what? They are happy AF to work for you, even during the difficult times. Because Kick-Ass, High-Functioning, Happy AF teams rise above difficulty rather than dwelling on it, so that you can keep moving forward together no matter what happens.

Developing, strengthening and flexing your C.O.R.E. can make you that leader. Don't you want that for yourself and your team? I know you do, that's why you are here. I am going to teach you about each section of your Leadership C.O.R.E. in this book and show you how to use it to close conflict and develop that Kick-Ass, High-Functioning, Happy AF team that you've been dreaming about.

The One Thing That Can Stop You: FEAR.

We internalize conflict as something to be feared because it is often introduced as negative or invisible, or something not to talk about or learn from. When this fear makes an appearance, it shows up with an arsenal of ways for shutting down conversation. It offers us the chance to choose from making demands, answering endless questions meant to sidetrack us, issuing ultimatums, judging, threatening, jumping to conclusions, lecturing or not entertaining the conversation at all. When we operate in this space, we are choosing to lead from a place that is unsure or downright mistrustful of what conflict has to offer.

The other side of that fear is presented in the work that I am laying out here. I teach leaders how to use their mindset and skillset to resolve conflicts, and that encompasses a wide range of things: communication, contemplative practices, negotiation, mediation, social and emotional learning and the one thing that almost everyone is afraid to discuss… diversity.

The fear of having to explore your conflict story and triggers and learn to bring conflict closer in order to engage in the hard conversations, can be enough to make you put down this book right now or fling it into your 'I'll get to it later/never pile.' Add to the mix the role diversity plays in communication and conflict and some of you may get frustrated and think that it is too much to learn. You may be ready to give up on the idea that you can master the art of conflict. Don't do that.

Don't let fear of conflict and communication stop you from being the kind of leader who understands that conflict comes with leadership and business and that Bold Leaders are there to meet conflict with skill, confidence and power. The leaders who can show up like that every time for themselves and their team are going to be at the forefront of leadership and financial success. Believe me, I want that to be you and here's why.

The Cost of Hidden Conflict

I'm just going to come right out and say this. The biggest cost of hidden conflict is that you are constantly stressed out about the fact that if anyone finds out what is really going on behind the scenes in your company, they will know that you are perpetrating leadership fraud. That's right, you are posing as a leader and it all looks pretty to the outside world, but the truth is that your team is too frightened of you to tell you when they don't understand something and they are making costly, time-consuming mistakes. Or some of your team members are unhappy and are expressing that behind your back and creating dissention, division and real unhappiness within the company.

Hidden conflict shows up in so many ways including snide comments at meetings, silence at meetings when you ask if there are any questions, launches and big projects that are not successful unless you step in because your team is not cohesive and cannot handle the stress. (I've got plenty more examples but you know your truth.)

If you are an avoider of conflict then I can promise you that none of this is going away. If you are a yeller, I can guarantee that your team will either yell back or at each other or worse, retreat and take their complaints with them and everyone will be frustrated, unhappy and unproductive.

If you are a leader who just wants everyone to get along and you have tried to be friendly and a good listener and please everyone, let me be straight with you, that is not what leadership looks like to your team and they are either taking advantage of you or secretly viewing you as someone they cannot respect.

Inevitably, your clients will start to see what's really going on behind the curtain and you cannot yell, avoid or peace your way out of that.

The Hidden Cost of Not Understanding The Role of Culture

Bold Leaders understand that communication is a two-way street, both externally and internally. What I mean by this is that, when it comes to communication, leaders need to place as much importance on what is happening inside of themselves and the other person/people involved as they do on what is coming out of their mouths or what their body language is saying. Inside of us our conflict stories are shaped by culture and experiences. The way we communicate is more of a cultural experience. There are many of us who are in touch with that fact daily, especially if conflict is involved. As a leader, you have to develop an understanding for cultural diversity and the impact it has on communication and conflict or you will miss many important cues that tell you that your people are having problems. You will also lose valuable team members who's culturally influenced communication styles of silence, unfiltered "speaking their truth, directness or hiding their true feelings were either misinterpreted as problematic or never effectively addressed.

The Conflict Closer Weighs In: Meet *Tamara

Tamara is part of a dynamic team of very successful and very driven leaders. Tamara's conflict story didn't just carry the message that conflict is bad, but that every culture has its rules. As a girl, she learned that her voice was not as important as boy's voices. As part of her ethnicity, she learned that she could not be true to her culture if she spoke up during conflict and made her feelings and thoughts known.

I helped her work through those cultural barriers/conflict stories and in a short time she began feeling more powerful and using the skills to begin to speak about ideas and problems happening with the team and her boss. She also realized that even though it felt like it, she was not betraying her culture by using these skills. She was still who she was culturally and had many ways to exhibit that in her life. The biggest result was that her boss saw the change and how it benefited Tamara, the team and the company and promoted her several times.

Tamara's conflict story is replicated among many people, and as a leader, while you can't possibly know every story, you need to come to the table understanding that leading a diverse team means that culture is going to play a substantial role in both communication and conflict.

The Benefits of Uncovering and Closing Hidden Conflict

In my work I have seen it all, I mean every kind of leader imaginable and the bottom line is, when you lead in a way that does not take the time to develop a healthy, skillful and productive relationship with conflict then you are unnecessarily stressed and much less powerful. That means your team is wasting a lot of time, costing you a lot of money and much less likely to be loyal or careful, and carelessness affects work climate and profits. You can't fire your way out of this either or it will be an endless turnover and the problems will still remain. That's not what you want. You don't want more of any of this. That's why you're still reading.

You want to be the happy, less stressed, **Bold Leader** of a highly successful and profitable business with a Kick-Ass, High-Functioning Happy AF to work for you Team. A team that's loyal to your business all day, every day. That means you have to start right now to uncover and address the "not so hidden" hidden conflict in your company so that you can close those conflicts.

So, let's get to work on your **Leadership C.O.R.E.**

Chapter 2

Communication Is Not The Key, It Is The Door

As I said earlier, conflict is about communication. As leaders, you are always communicating. Therefore, it is your job to be as clear, as concise, as firm, as confident and as skilled as possible. When it comes to communication and conflict you want and need to be at the top of your game, because it is the door to opening up courageous conversation and closing conflict.

With so many teams working virtually, and with a variety of ways of communicating other than in person, the need for highly skilled communicators is increasing, especially in times of conflict. When conflict rears its head, people either get loud or silent. Few people have the skills to manage it well. That is why your team is looking to you as the leader to be fearless during these situations. When conflict arises fearlessness starts with *the way* and *the when* you start communicating. Both are equally important.

I'll talk about **the way** in a minute let's talk about **the when. The when** sets the stage for allowing people to be more at ease with conflict. If you have gained a reputation for ignoring or avoiding even the smallest disagreements, then your team will always be fearful and resentful of conflict and eventually, of you. I want you to be the kind of leader that not only expects conflict to show up at your door but is always ready to engage in it by communicating the hell out of it (literally).

Masterful communication can take the parts of conflict that everybody dreads and turn them into learning experiences for everyone involved. Granted, though it may never be a heavenly experience for folks, your leadership can help your team understand that it is natural, inevitable and manageable. Thus, stand tall when it shows up, do not go into hiding and do not go to the other extreme of yelling, interrupting, blaming, dismissing or name-calling.

I want you to really get it when I say: the more effectively we communicate, the less confused others become and the more the opportunities of getting to the genesis of what the conflict is about among your team members, whether the cause is within or outside the business. This requires a willingness to get close to both the people and the conflict. I'm not suggesting that you have to develop a friendship, but rather that you care about your team as people who want and need to be listened to, just like you do.

So now we get to *the way.* This starts with listening deeply and not just listening the way we normally do. You know what I mean. We are easily distracted during conversations. Listening deeply means that we are not **just** listening, but we are **mindfully** and **strategically** listening beneath the words in order to get to the source of the conflict.

Mindful Listening

Most people listen with their minds full. That is, they listen while thinking of other things like 'get to the point already,' 'why is this nonsense happening,' 'I need to get my point across here.' Any of this sound familiar?

If it's not that, then they are thinking about all of the things that they have to do besides listen. Mindful listening is not just the complete opposite of that but it is also intentional, interested and purposeful listening. While most of us don't engage in mindful listening, it is not that hard to learn, but it really does require a commitment to practicing it. As someone aspiring to be at the forefront of leadership, having this tool in your toolkit puts you head and shoulders above the rest while at the same time, gives you a huge return on your investment.

Yes, that's right, it is an investment of your time, but the better you get at it, the less time you waste, the more connected you and your team become and the better the work quality.

How do you mindfully listen?

First, have the intention to listen mindfully. That means that you should get rid of any potential distractions, especially if you are communicating via the phone or on a video call instead of in person. The temptation to do something other than listen is intense when the other person cannot see you. You therefore really have to commit to it.

The next step is to listen without judgment. You will get judgmental thoughts, we all do, but you should not let these thoughts steer you away from listening deeply and take you off to a place of blaming and assuming that you know what's really going on or deciding that they are wrong.

Resist the urge to interrupt them. This is one of the hardest things to do for so many of us, especially if you are a leader. First of all, this is the way that most of us listen. We listen up to the point where we want to interrupt to either disagree or get our point across. It's an encouraged habit, particularly in business where too much talking is seen as a waste of time. Secondly, as leaders, we are either too quick to pull the authority card: 'I don't have time to listen to this,' 'I'm the boss so just do it my way,' or we want to avoid hearing just how big a mess this really is so we cut our team off and tell them to find a way to work it out.

Next, you want to listen deeply and beneath their words. What are they not saying? From their perspective, what is this conflict about? If you know them well, you want to try and analyze the conflict from their perspective. If you are just getting to know them, you want to lean in even more to try and understand them and their point of view. This is when Strategic listening starts to come into play.

Strategic Listening

Listening strategically means you are focusing on the key things that lead to better understanding of what someone is saying to you.

You are listening for the content. In other words, what is the problem?

You are listening for feelings; what emotions, both said and unsaid, are driving this situation?

You are listening for values; what are the important foundations shaping their perspectives in this particular situation? Do they value independence, trust, honesty? What about this situation is pushing up against their values?

The last thing you are listening for is positional statements. This aspect should not distract you. Positional statements often sound like threats or ultimatums. They give us the least information about what is really important to the person and the conflict. It either just tells us how limited their communication skills are or how high their frustration levels are at a particular point. Positional statements are often meant to scare, block, stall, expose or harm in some way. "Well maybe I should just quit!", "Maybe you should get someone else to do this since you are so unhappy with my work" are both examples of positional statements.

Conversations, particularly conflict conversations, predominantly center around the first three areas: content, feelings and values. If you want to get good at closing conflict as a leader, you need to learn how to master these three aspects. You also need to become proficient at noting the positional statements in your mind and listening past them to get to the real information. Most conflicts are derailed by positional statements because they push our buttons and trigger us to react rather than respond to the important parts of a conversation. We will talk more about triggers and reactions versus response in Chapter 4.

These listening skills are incredibly powerful and when used properly, they can give you valuable insight into the person and the conflict. They also strengthen connections and create safety. That inspires confidence in you as a leader. When your team experiences this kind of listening, they know that they are valued. When you invest your valuable time in them, it shows that you not only care about profits, but also about your people. They also know that resolving the day to day issues that come up is a priority for you, which, frankly translates, to 'less mess means less stress' for everybody, even you.

Responding Effectively

You've listened deeply. Now, it's time to respond.

Your investment in listening should have given you enough information to reflect. Yes, I am asking you not to respond the second they are done talking.

Instead pause, take it all in and then tell them what you have heard and understood. You need to lay out the content, values and feelings.

Remember, some of this is unsaid. When you engage in mindful and strategic listening, you are listening to both what they are saying and what is beneath the words. People don't often share their values or all of their feelings, but you can learn to hear them if you are faithful to practicing the listening skills.

Once you've summarized for them what you heard and understood, you should give them a check-in statement. You can say, "did I get that right?" or "is that what's happening here?" This shows them that you have in fact been listening and gives them the opportunity to confirm that you have heard them correctly or that you've missed the point.

If you've missed it, of course you are going to need to ask them to fill you in on where you got it wrong. If you've gotten it right, then you can move on.

This is the part where you can ask for more information to give you a fuller picture or you can share your thoughts on the situation. The key here is to lay out your thoughts in relation to what they have shared as well as what will serve the best interests of the team and the business.

Remember earlier on when I told you that I led a Kick-Ass, High-Functioning, Happy AF team? I made many mistakes while working with them. However, by continually using and mastering these skills, I was able to increase connection among the team members while increasing productivity and our value to the company. I am so grateful for these skills!

My job as a leader began with one trainer on my team and a shared administrative assistant. One year later, I had to hire and supervise 6 additional trainers and a new assistant. We were a very tight-knit, creative, fun, caring and highly-successful team who worked together for many years. We all genuinely enjoyed the work and our time together. I took the chance to sharpen my skills and learn from my mistakes while leading this team that was literally thrust on me due to the success of our work and an influx of funding. Believe me, as successful as I was in resolving conflicts, I was just as successful in making mistakes. I think it would be useful to share one that illustrates the listening and responding skills in this chapter.

The Conflict Closer Weighs In: Meet My Mistake

One of my team members was a passionate and skilled young man who seldom held his tongue about anything. He was most certainly the first one to express his frustrations against any policies or expectations that the company and I had for the team. I knew the importance of meeting regularly to hash out ideas, learn new skills, connect on a personal level and to voice successes and frustrations. In those meetings he was most passionate about his frustrations. Since I was the leader, most of his frustrations were directed at me. During one particular meeting, he ranted off a list of frustrations that quite frankly, were identical to many of the things that challenged me on a regular basis. Instead of employing my skills to reign in the numerous emotions triggered in me by his rant, I looked around the room at the rest of the team with what I am sure was a smirk and then looked him dead in the eye and said, "welcome to my world."

I did not acknowledge his feelings or values or even the content of what he was putting on the table. Just a smart- ass reaction from his boss, because I, too, was frustrated and because as the boss, I could react in any way I wanted. Hell, I

45

*could have walked off and ended the meeting if I
wanted to; I knew I had the power.*

*Well, he exploded, which of course escalated the
conflict. That meant that I had to spend even more
time with him, this time in my office. But I chose to
approach it differently, I used the tools of mindful
and strategic listening to de-escalate his feelings of
frustration, overwhelm, under-appreciation and fear
that our clients were not getting the services they
required. I validated his values of excellence, self-
care, honesty, fairness and justice. I responded by
stating what was possible and what could be
created and what simply could not be changed. I
even apologized for my reaction during the meeting
and he apologized as well. After that conversation
he remained a passionate and highly productive
member of our team who did not complain as much
and I was not triggered as often by his complaints
because I understood the values and feelings they
represented.*

I know that it may feel like giving time and attention
to your team and conflicts is stressful, but once you
commit to: using these skills regularly,
understanding your team, and communicating
more effectively, you will start to see how engaging
in conversations early enough to prevent or close

the door on conflict actually relieves your stress. It is so worth it.

I am giving you permission to put the book down right now and take in everything you just read. It's a lot to take in and think about putting into practice. If you can already see why my clients hire me and want to do the same or if you have questions, reach out to me at mailto:lynne@lynnemaureenhurdle.com Then pick the book up and dive back in!

Chapter 3

Objectivity, Your Hidden Strength

Strengthening this part of your core is like lying on the floor, going in to crunch position, taking both feet off the floor, stretching your legs and arms straight out in front of you and holding that position.

It takes everything in you; you have to be aware that every part of your body is involved in this exercise. You have to breathe and hold back from breaking that position and collapsing on the floor. The same applies when you are developing your **Objectivity** muscles. You have to take in everything happening within the conflict situation, be able to skillfully respond and then step back from the situation in order to objectively look at yourself in relationship to the conflict and how you perceived it, contributed to it and can grow from it.

I thought it best to show you this element of your **C.O.R.E.** through some examples of conflicts my clients have asked for my assistance in. For each of these situations, I coached my clients to have an Objective Reflection Response - essentially assessing their response after the conflict conversation has taken place.

Micro-Managing Conflicts

Letting go and allowing others to work or even answer a call or an email on your behalf is determined by how well you have trained them, your communication with them, as well as trust and self-reflection. Often, when a leader finds themselves checking every report, email, project or type of communication, there is a hidden trigger that they must uncover within themselves or there will be resentment and discontent among their team.

Skillful Response: Communicating the company mission, company style and reputation and the need for all things to be consistent with that of everyone else is important. Ask questions, ask for clarifications and, if need be, suggest more training. Express the confidence you have in them and own up to micro-managing. Go do what you have assigned yourself to do and start learning to trust them.

Objective Reflection Response: What is distrustful leadership? What is one step I can take to let go and trust? What's my best guess as to the root cause of distrust on my part?

Cultural Differences Conflicts

Bold leaders examine the conflicts created by the

cultural norms of the workplace and create conversations about them. Culture plays a distinct and big role in how we do things, what we think, believe, hear and/or see and yet, not enough attention is paid to it. If your team is in conflict about workstyles, it may be as a result of cultural differences. This can hold up productivity, prevent cohesiveness and at the same time, go undetected because of assumptions and lack of knowledge.

Bold Response: Be committed to leading a diverse team and state that as a purposeful intention of yours because of all the good it brings to the company. Acknowledge the work that it will take to build a harmonious team that works well together and then set up a conversation to talk about workstyles and their relationship to culture. Consult expert materials, podcasts, and conversations and prepare yourself to use them as resources with the team.

Objective Reflection Response: Be honest with yourself about your own knowledge in this area. What are your fears about taking this on and why are these fears coming up for you? Breathe and then decide on a first step for the first of many conversations.

Workstyle Conflicts

People have different workstyles, which may not always be related to culture. When you have 2 type A's, one laid back and another 'leave me alone so I can work in peace' team members, it can present challenges, not only for you, but also for each of them as well. What happens when you find that even the type A's are being competitive instead of collaborative?

Bold Response: Of course, when creating a team, you want to create dialogue among them about their work styles and how they may complement each other. You also need to inform them of how their work styles can potentially create conflict. But if the problem is already here, you'll want to bring the people in conflict together and mediate the conflict. Help them put solutions in place and make sure there is a plan to revisit this and discuss progress and any setbacks. Expect that difference can create conflict, so get ahead of it by instituting ongoing opportunities for checking in and problem-solving, both together and separately.

Objective Reflection Response: What is your work style and what are the ways that it complements and causes friction? Yes, you are the leader, so you have the final say, but looking into yourself gives you insight in to others.

Gossip and Complaints Behind Your Back

This is not about social media; this is about folks sitting in the meetings or having conversations with you and assuring you that everything is going fine with them and their work when in reality, they are actually creating a toxic environment by gossiping about you and/or others and complaining about their work, the culture and the company.

Bold Response: You have to get right to it and speak directly about this to the people who are engaging in this behavior. Be clear about the company culture that is being built and provide an opportunity for them to offer up their complaints to you. Be firm about what is not acceptable or useful, specifically with regard to gossiping and not directing complaints to you. Set clear boundaries and expectations for future behavior and keep your ear to the ground without micro-managing.

Objective Reflection Response: Set aside some time for silence and to get grounded in your purpose and the kind of culture you are determined to create. Tune in to the possibility that you are giving off the vibe of someone who is not approachable and is to be feared. Think about who might give you objective insight on this.

Objectivity strengthens your ability to listen longer and deeper. It allows you time for a more thoughtful response and a wider perspective on the situation, your team and yourself. Closing conflict becomes easier when a leader can respond skillfully and objectively. Your ability to see more potential solutions and encourage your team to be creative in this area is heightened by your ability to be objective during conflict.

Chapter 4

Resolving Conflicts Through Courageous Conversations

Leaders of Kick-Ass, High-Functioning, Happy AF teams are not just talking it out. They are hosting courageous conversations with conflict resolution as their goal.

The Conflict Closer Weighs In: Meet *Thomas

*Thomas phoned me one day about a powerful leadership opportunity that had been handed to him unexpectedly. He signed on to be second in command but was suddenly handed the job of head leader in charge instead. He was fearful but decided to push forward anyway.

He reached out, because he had been given the heads up that he was walking into a storm and he wanted to develop a leadership strategy for navigating through the 'storm' and making sure that everyone not only survived but thrived under his leadership.

Through our strategy, Thomas was able to hear the real issues of personality conflicts, an unclarified mission, a team that did not feel heard or valued and a great deal of previously undisclosed fear to be taking on such a huge project together. Because of the work we did together he took on these huge conflicts and was able to circumvent high turnover. He was recognized not only by management for his leadership, but by his team who felt he was committed to not only the company, but their concerns as well.

Bold Leadership recognizes the need to choose to lead into and through a storm. Unfortunately, in business, when it comes to conflict, because most leaders are not prepared at the start, they often let it build into a storm and then they are eventually left to watch as it grows into a full-blown hurricane. At this point, most leaders want to run and hide or at least go someplace and scream, "Why Me????"

Getting to the other side of conflict with everyone intact and ready to sail the ship to safe, happy and productive shores together requires a leader who knows how to purposefully lead in to the storm. This is where your mindset about conflict begins to set the stage for how you will guide your team, manage the conflict and come through to the other side together.

Mindset

Expect Conflict.

That means, stop trying to avoid it, stop dreading it, just know that conflict comes with people and business and since it is already here, you are going to need to handle it.

Skill Up!

Keep this book handy. Refer to it before you engage in any conflict. Review any other techniques you have mastered that are effective.

Conflict is Here to Teach You About You.

No matter how much you learn about other people during a conflict, what conflict really does is give you real insight into what triggers you, how you manage it and what effect your conflict management style has on your team. Be open to learning all of that. Commit to using this opportunity to get to know conflict better and to get to know yourself in conflict better. This is all part of developing a relationship with it and storms allow us to get intimate with conflict because you have to be all in as a leader in order to make it through.

Engage

The First Thing You Have to Do is to Level with Yourself.

You are in a storm, there is no getting out of it because as the leader, unless you inherited it, you likely played a role in causing it. Whether you avoided it or ignited it, it is happening on your watch and now you have to not only handle it, but you also have to engage in it with skill. The moment is right now.

Embrace Resistance.

Understand that both relief and resistance usually exist within a storm. People are afraid, angry, resentful, confused, unsure and a whole host of other emotions and they are tossing them all in your direction. As much as they want the conflict to be resolved, they also have their own reasons for participating in it. By embracing resistance, you are fully expecting it. You can then prepare yourself to listen to other people's perspectives on what is happening on a deeper level. Resistance isn't created to go against you personally. It is, however, personal for those involved. They need their questions answered, their fears heard and their requests validated through mindful and strategic listening.

Account for Your Own Actions.

Resolving conflict requires leaders to look within and identify where their triggers lie. You also need to prepare yourself to be triggered. Remember my personal story about how, after my mom's death, I took the time to delve into my own relationship with conflict and how it had been shaped by my upbringing? Remember you too have your own conflict story that has left its own wounds. Particularly during storms those wounds get triggered by certain people, words and scenarios. You need to develop an awareness of what's being triggered and the effect it is having on you and you have to keep it in check, because during a storm, your team is in reaction mode and they need you to be ready to respond rather than react.

You need to remain calm enough to prepare an appropriate response. If, as the leader, you are confronted with how your actions contributed to or even led to the blowing up of things, consider the possibility that there is truth there.

When we react, we are letting our feelings dictate our words and actions. Responding means that you are able to manage the emotions that come with being triggered by releasing them and making good decisions about the situation you are faced with.

Responding means that you and not your feelings or past conflicts are in control.

If you are reacting, own it and then move on to responding and determining a course of action. Looking at the damage done and going for the easier fixes first can only be successful if you start to work on a course of action to resolve the larger conflicts. Involve all voices and consider as many solutions as possible before you determine the plan that you will move forward with.

Implement Your First Set of Actions.
Leading transparently throughout the conflict is critical to keeping everyone on board, together and connected to you, each other and the solutions proposed. Clearly, you are the leader, and if you want them to follow, they need you to let them in on as much as you can about what the plan is and how it will be implemented and their role and importance in it. Make sure that part of your plan includes leading in a way that empowers. Every hole is not yours to plug. Give your team the opportunity to resolve conflicts among themselves, either with your help as a mediator or by meeting together and discussing their issues.

Navigate, Negotiate, Navigate.
It's a dance, regardless of whether you don't like

conflict or dancing. You take a few steps forward and one step back. Everyone is not going to like everything, but being the bold leader that you are, listening and negotiating your way through the more difficult issues allows you to find out what is in the way and reshape the plan so that you can continue to navigate your way through the storm and find resolutions that will allow everyone to rebuild together.

The times that we are in require **Bold Leaders** who will use all of these skills in order to walk into the fire with confidence every time. I need you to be one of them.

Chapter 5

Executing Excellence Every Day

This is the last part of your C.O.R.E. It is about executing excellence every day and expecting the same from your team. Unfortunately, too many leaders expect top notch performance from their team but are unable to deliver it themselves in the areas outside of productivity.

Let's be honest here - there are many leaders who are bringing in a tremendous amount of money but are secretly pulling out their hair because they cannot get the results they want out of their team. Executing excellence every day means showing up ready to lead in a way that teaches you something significant about yourself so that you can be a good role model for your team, and that is all kinds of good news for your people, product and profits.

When it comes to closing conflict and making sure that your Kick-Ass, High-Functioning Happy AF philosophy works for your team, while at the same time keeping them inspired, motivated and ready to jump into the next great thing that you are going to do together, you need to model these things:

You Don't Have to Respond to Everything Bad That Someone Says About You

In other words, sometimes you just have to ignore what people say. With the popularity of social media, in particular Twitter, we are seeing leaders in every arena 'clapping back' at every remark made against them harder and faster. This is the opposite of what your team needs to feel; they need to feel safe to make mistakes and learn how to do their best for you and the business. **Bold Leadership** requires a higher skill level when managing feelings, triggers and reactions. People are often unhappy under the leadership of a person who doesn't know how to walk away or who just cannot let a remark go unanswered.

Do unto Others as You Would Have Them Do unto You

The best work climates are those where people feel respected and cared for and where leaders live by this rule. These leaders don't name-call, scream, berate and/or intimidate their team in order to get them to fear them and be more productive. The mistake often made by leaders is that they do the things that were done to them even though they hated it. Bold Leaders know that the very things they hate being done to them are the things that will cause resentment, dissatisfaction and a desire to leave the company.

Apologies Are a Necessary Part of The Work

My friend and colleague, Achim Nowak, in his advice to leaders in his "Energy Boost" blog, beautifully states,

"Self-awareness is not a luxury item, it is a daily practice. Impactful leaders are mindful and willing to self-correct."

Apologies are hard work, even for those of us who don't find it that difficult to apologize. Saying the words is the easy part. The difficulty lies in the work that we need to do in order to get us to the place where we realize that we need to apologize. The key to apologies is knowing and remembering that most conflicts, misunderstandings and feelings often set up the need for an apology. Be prepared to examine your own mindset, words, beliefs and actions whenever you are involved in a conflict because the apology may need to come from you. If so, keep in mind that with so much negative stigma attached to saying the words "I'm sorry" and "I apologize," you may not want or need to lead with an apology. In conversation people want to know that they have been heard and that you can recognize you're wrong from their point of view.

Reflecting their words back to them and then apologizing at the end can be even more heart-felt because an understanding has been established.

In my earlier story about Dan Gilbert, when he apologized, the end result was reportedly an extra $100 million for getting LeBron back, but the real benefit was a repaired relationship and personal growth for both. I want all of that for you too.

Look for Meaning in Your Words and Actions
"Meaning is the lens through which we understand our experiences and the link through which we connect with each other," Kate O'Neill in The Meaningful Manifesto.

Doing the work to understand the meaning of your actions and words allows you to leave room for the possibility that you may not know the true meaning of other's words and actions. Most people look at making mistakes and getting into conflict as a bad thing that must be avoided at all costs. When in fact digging deep in to the untapped wisdom in conflict allows us to find the meaning behind the conditioned responses that we've come to believe are our true selves in conflict. Society has taught us that looking within and finding meaning behind our words and actions makes our leadership look weak. Buying into these beliefs has taken you away from the wisdom that lies within you and prevented you from being the powerful, impactful, influential, skilled, confident, **Bold Leader** that you are here to be. Until now…

If you really want to close conflict you must lead from your **C.O.R.E.** and you will not only get the results that you want from your team, but you will also see the amazing difference in yourself.

Conclusion

You just read all of these juicy points and what I know is that most of you will put this book down and decide that it is easier to just continue hiding the conflict in your business. But don't do that because when you step up and take this on here's what will happen for you. Conflict will no longer be something that you dread. It may not be your favorite thing but you will start to see it as something that is here to teach you some important things about yourself and others. You will discover that the things you think are so definite about the way that you approach and handle conflict are actually fluid and adaptable to a new mindset and skillset. You will start to see positive change in yourself and your team just by using Chapter 1 skillfully and consistently. If you apply what I am teaching in this book you will want more because it will be clear to you that being a **Bold Leader** in conflict is what is missing in leadership and it is exactly what you want to be.

So what are you going to do? Are you going to continue to stick all your fingers in the dam trying to keep all this unresolved conflict from sinking the company? Are you going to continue to be stressed out because of miscommunication, lack of communication, endless arguments, minimum productivity and hidden resentment and discontent? Or are you going to decide that you are ready to go after **Bold Leadership** by Closing Conflict and Developing a Kick-Ass, High-Functioning, Happy AF Team?

If you are saying Yes to using this book as a beginning step to that kind of **Bold Leadership** then here are 5 next steps you can take.

1. Use the Communication chapter as a constant guide. Apply it, Apply it, Apply it.
2. Commit to discovering your conflict stories and create an awareness about the triggers that those stories have set up for you.
3. Become a **Bold Leader** and ask for feedback on how these skills are landing with your team.
4. Keep referring back to the book and the specific parts that feed your progress.
5. Reach out to me. Let me know how its going for you.

The world of business needs you at your best in conflict because conflict is not going away, so, the **Bold Leader** that can masterfully sail the ship in to and through the storm to the sunshine that awaits on the other side, **WINS!**

Thank you for reading this book. I honor your desire to do the hard work of Closing Conflict in order to be the best **Bold Leader** that you can be.

Lynne

How to Work with The Conflict Closer

When you are ready to be that **Bold Leader** that you know you want to be then you are ready to maximize the effects of reading this book by taking advantage of the many ways that you, your company and your team can learn **my Leadership C. O.R.E. Program**. **One on one coaching** is a great way to learn and deepen these skills. **I also offer in-person seminars, keynotes for conferences**, or you can bring me in to do a series of **Leadership C.O.R.E**. workshops with you and your team.

I work with High-Achieving Leaders who lead teams. By diagnosing the problem areas, **I help you, your company and your team tighten up your C.O.R.E.**

Communication
Objectivity
Resolving Conflicts
Executing Excellence

Go from reacting to responding to finally resolving conflict.

Get ready to build and strengthen your Leadership C.O.R.E. with me.

Learn more at buildleadershipcore.com

And then contact me at
lynne@lynnemaureenhurdle.com

Website: www.lynnemaureenhurdle.com

LinkedIn: /lynnemaureenhurdle

Facebook: /theconflictcloser

Facebook Group: /groups/soulofconflict

TEDx Talk:
https://lynnemaureenhurdle.com/about-lynne/

About Lynne Maureen Hurdle

Lynne Maureen Hurdle is a conflict resolution strategist, facilitator, speaker, and coach who blends the connection between communication, conflict and culture in to her unique style of engagement for leaders. Prevention, Intervention and Transformational Conflict Resolution are at the heart of her work. She engages her clients with the infusion of creative processes designed to create dialogue and teach skills that can be used in the most difficult leadership situations.

The belief that helping people transform their lives begins with transforming your own, led to her well received TEDx talk entitled "The Weight of Hate." She is the creator of The Soul of Conflict Summit, a groundbreaking online forum designed to create deep dialogue around conflict, old wounds and healing. She writes about Breaking Culture:

71

Conflict and Cultural Breakthroughs for Psychology Today.

She has spent the last thirty years delivering her unique trainings, workshops and deep coaching to leaders from Harlem to Hong Kong and from the South Bronx to South Africa. She brings a wealth of knowledge, experience and her special "Lynnergy" to every client.

Acknowledgements

Jennifer Griner, thank you for all the edits, last minute corrections, formatting, cover creation, excitement and love that you put in to this. So grateful to have you on my team.

Kathy Kidd, without your encouragement at such a difficult time this book would not have been written when it was needed.

Jennifer Kem, you were the voice that said "leaders need you to write this book now. They need to know what you know about conflict."

Achim Nowak, your encouragement to do this work as my own boss in my own way started this entrepreneur journey. Who else would I ask to write the foreward but you?

Sarah Paikai, your courage to look at yourself and do the work is inspiring on so many levels. It is wonderful to see your hard work paying off.

Debbie Burns, your encouragement and insightful edits were just what was needed for this book to happen. Thank you for trusting my gifts.

Joe Burns you get me and the work and why leaders have to change their relationship with conflict.

Kathy Goughenour, from the first session and the aha moments that kept coming, I knew I was on to something. Thank you for your confidence in me.

Gisele Bonds and Andy Richter you are both super talented photographers as evidenced by the cover photos.

Made in United States
North Haven, CT
14 November 2021

11135223R10042